Publication Design by Amanda Jane Jones
Cover photograph by Jessica Peterson

weldon**owen**

415 Jackson Street, Suite 200,
San Francisco, CA 94111
Telephone: 415 291 0100
Fax: 415 291 8841
www.wopublishing.com

Weldon Owen is a division of

BONNIER

KINFOLK

SUBSCRIBE

VISIT WWW.KINFOLKMAG.COM/SUBSCRIBE

FOUR VOLUMES EACH YEAR

CONTACT US

If you have any questions or comments,
email us at *info@kinfolkmag.com*

SUBSCRIPTIONS

For questions regarding your subscription,
email *subscribe@kinfolkmag.com*

STOCKISTS

If you would like to carry *Kinfolk*,
email us at *distribution@kinfolkmag.com*

SUBMISSIONS

Send all submissions to
submissions@kinfolkmag.com

EDITOR

To reach the editor,
please email *nathan@kinfolkmag.com*

WWW.KINFOLKMAG.COM

WELCOME

We are interested in why we cook and eat together, and in the people, relationships, and social elements that keep us inviting company into our homes.

As you will soon find out, this magazine is about more than cooking and eating. We are interested in why we cook and eat together, and in the people, relationships, and social elements that keep us inviting company into our homes. We're simplifying what seems to be an increasingly complicated and intimidating concept: entertaining. Even the word sounds stiff and formal, when in reality it's quite simple, and we do it all the time. We don't need a week's notice, seating charts, name cards—we don't even need a meal.

Understandably, at times, we all enjoy the novelty of the extravagant—the centerpieces, appetizers, pom poms, and elaborate tissue paper installations—but let's not allow the elaborate to keep us from those low-key, no-fuss gatherings in between. This volume includes personal stories about gathering during the fall and winter months: morning walks, using natural candlelight, escaping with friends for a weekend retreat in the mountains or on the coast, and revisiting nostalgic traditions—in short, being in the moment with the elements and people around us. This is a place to share ideas and inspiration for those simple get-togethers and moments. Because *that* is what we're about.

While it may sound audacious, I'd like to suggest that there is a proper—or most effective—way to read this magazine. The images, stories, and ideas are simply not conducive to a quick peruse. Many feel that with a magazine, a quick flip-through will suffice, but in our case, the opposite is true. Set aside some quiet time in the evening to read this volume, to curl up with a blanket and soak it all in.

NATHAN WILLIAMS, EDITOR OF KINFOLK MAGAZINE

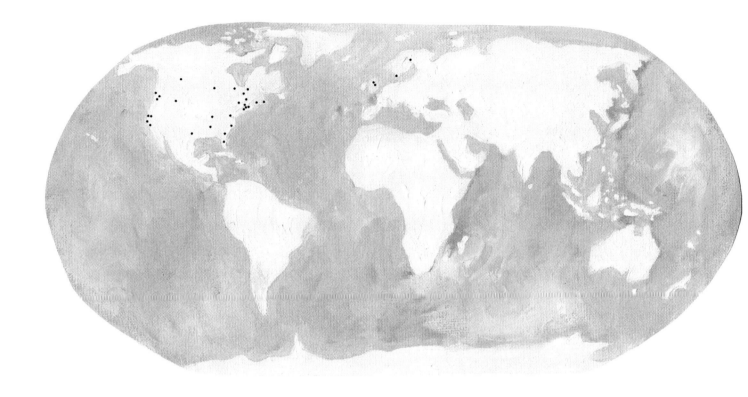

NATHAN WILLIAMS
Portland, Oregon
Editor

AMANDA JANE JONES
Ann Arbor, Michagan
Designer

ERICA MIDKIFF
Homewood, Alabama
Copy Editor

HEIDI SWANSON
San Francisco, California
Photographer & Writer

ANDREW GALLO
Arlington, Virginia
Film Maker

ARIEL DEARIE
Brooklyn, New York
Florist

ANDREA GENTL
Brookyln, New York
Photographer

CARISSA GALLO
Arlington, Virginia
Photographer

ANDREW STEWART
Brooklyn, New York
Stylist

BRIAN FERRY
London, United Kingdom
Photographer & Writer

KIMBERLEY HASSELBRINK
San Francisco, CA
Writer

NIKAELA PETERS
Manitoba, Canada
Writer

KATIE STRATTON
Dayton, Ohio
Painter

ALICE GAO
Brooklyn, New York
Photographer

TEC PETAJA
Nashville, Tennesse
Photographer

ANAIS WADE
Los Angeles, California
Photographer & Writer

JEWELS OF NEW YORK
Brooklyn, New York
Prop & Food Stylists

CHELSEA PETAJA
Nashville, Tennesse
Stylist

DAX HENRY
Los Angeles, California
Photographer & Writer

ALEXIS SIEMONS
Philadelphia, PA
Writer

ELISE YETTON
Nashville, Tennesse
Writer

CATHERINE SEARLE-WILLIAMS
Portland, Oregon
Writer

DAVID WINWARD
Salt Lake City, Utah
Writer

SARAH WINWARD
Salt Lake City, Utah
Writer

CHELSEA FUSS
Portland, Oregon
Stylist

LISA WARNINGER
Portland, Oregon
Photographer

LEO PATRONE
Salt Lake City, Utah
Photographer

HILDA GRAHNAT
Sweden
Photographer

SARAH BRITTON
Copenhagen, Denmark
Writer

NIKOLE HERRIOTT
Toronto, Canada
Stylist & Writer

LAURA D'ART
Portland, Oregon
Photographer

JULIE POINTER
Portland Oregon
Writer

EMMA ROBERTSON
Dallas, Texas
Stylist

JULIE WALKER
Salt Lake City, Utah
Writer

TIGER IN A JAR
Salt Lake City, Utah
Film Makers

JESSICA PETERSON
Salt Lake City, Utah
Photographer

WILLIAM HEREFORD
Brooklyn, New York
Photographer

LOU MORA
Los Angeles, California
Photographer

AUSTIN M. SAILSBURY
Orlando, Florida
Writer

TIM ROBISON
North Carolina
Photographer

JASON HUDSON
Toronto, Canada
Photographer

ASHLEY DENTON
Toronto, Canada
Food Stylist & Writer

YOUNGNA PARK
Brooklyn, New York
Photographer

LYNN RUSSELL
Corvallis, Oregon
Writer

JENNIFER CAUSEY
Brooklyn, New York
Photographer

MICHAEL MULLER
Brooklyn, New York
Photographer

KRISTIN TEIG
Boston, Massachusetts
Photographer

CHARLOTTE BLAND
London, United Kingdom
Photographer & Writer

SAER RICHARDS
Brooklyn, New York
Writer

REBECCA PARKER
Richmond, Virginia
Writer

TARA O'BRADY
St. Catharines, Canada
Writer

MICHAEL GRAYDON
Toronto, Canada
Photographer

RINNE ALLEN
Athens, Georgia
Photographer

WAYNE BREMSER
San Francisco
Photographer

BRITT CHUDLEIGH
Salt Lake City
Photographer

AMOS LANKA
Portland, Oregon
Photographer

EDEN LANG
Calgary, Canada
Photographer

MARTIN HYERS
Brookyln, New York
Photographer

JILLIAN GUYETTE
Rochester, New York
Photographer

PAIGE APPEL
Los Angeles, California
Stylist

KELLY HARRIS
Los Angeles, California
Stylist

ADELAIDE BROWN
North Carolina
Stylist

JAQUILYN AND TRAVIS SHUMATE
Tacoma, Washington
Photographers

FEW

ONE

ENTERTAINING FOR ONE

○

EMBRACING WINTER

PHOTOGRAPHS AND WORDS BY HEIDI SWANSON AND WAYNE BREMSER

I look forward to the cozy drama of winter — blustery storms, fat raindrops, hearty soups by candlelight, thick tights, and thicker sweaters.

The definition between seasons in San Francisco isn't always clear. You have to watch and listen to know winter is coming—but don't rely on the sky, which will tell you it's winter in summer, and summer in fall. There are other ways to tell that colder weather is mulling in the distance. The days start to get shorter, and not long after, if you look in doorways and alcoves, you'll see huge spider webs clinging to the Victorian curlicues and candy-colored moldings. At one point or another, each year, I walk right into the first sign of the changing seasons.

Around the same time you'll see Gravenstein apples cozying up to black Brandywine tomatoes at the farmers' markets, and I start to imagine all the things I want to do with the acorn and delicata squash that aren't far off. You'll see clothing shop windows around town shift their displays from chiffon to wool, and construction and painting crews become decreasingly visible, their scaffolding eventually disappearing entirely. I look forward to the cozy drama of winter—blustery storms, fat raindrops, hearty soups by candlelight, thick tights, and thicker sweaters. All of it.

Inside the house, my oven starts to find its groove again. Scents shift away from bright flashes of herby green and peppy hits of garlic, transitioning to deep, earthy baritones of roasted roots and rosemary. Soups and stews simmer, wines get fuller-bodied, festivities with friends are more frequent, and before you know it, it's time to reflect on another year's passing.

I have a list of things (both small and large) I want to do this season, before the year winds down entirely. I want to try a new soup recipe each week. Snowshoe to a backcountry cabin for a night. Make homemade holiday gifts rather than purchase them. Take my nephew puddle jumping in knee-high galoshes. Get to know the handful of root vegetables I typically ignore, which means choosing parsnips over potatoes, and kohlrabi over kale. Host a fondue night where friends bring fat platters of tasty ingredients to dunk. Bundle up near my biggest window with a pile of fiction. Daydream about a tropical getaway. And watch for the quiet signs that yet another favorite season is not far off in the distance.

CANDLES AND WINTER LIGHT

I resist the urge to turn on all of the lights at home. Instead, I light my candles.

If you visited my apartment on a winter's night, you would see tall white unscented candles in dishes, the melted wax forming irregular shapes and the flames casting changing light patterns against the walls and ceiling. The candles are perched on windowsills and countertops and tables, and they even sit next to me as I stand in the kitchen and chop vegetables for dinner. You see, as the days shorten and the world seems to be in a near-constant state of darkness, I resist the urge to turn on all of the lights at home. Instead, I light my candles.

I have always been very sensitive to light—I wait until the last possible minute to flip the switch and turn on electric lights. I do this in the summer when the days are long and the light stays around until 9:30 p.m. But I also do this in the winter, despite the short days and the afternoon sunsets. Even once the lights are switched on, I rarely use overhead lights because I find them harsh and unforgiving. Instead, smaller lamps are better suited to my (very particular) lighting needs.

In the winter, my relationship to light necessarily changes. The quality of light is different at this time of year — it feels colder, flatter, diffused, blue. Winter light changes our behavior and our moods, too. I sleep more, stay at home more often, and my mornings are especially groggy. Light is seasonal, fleeting and ephemeral. Just as we change the foods we eat in the winter, I think it is important to change other habits, too. Candlelight recognizes this change in my environment and allows me to make peace with it. Instead of resisting those long winter nights, I try to embrace them. As the day fades and dusk settles, it is nice to ease into the darkness of night by lighting a few candles. It feels more natural to me than turning on all of the lights in my apartment, and it is a ritual for the season and something I enjoy. The soft light is relaxing, warming, almost primitive.

It is easy to think that candles should be reserved for special occasions, dinner parties or romance—and I certainly think that they are especially appropriate at such times. However, in the winter I think that lighting candles is an everyday habit that can improve our quality of life. Living with more candlelight allows me to respect the change in seasons, to contemplate the coming of the darkness, and to enjoy the wait for the return of the sun.

PHOTOGRAPH BY ANDREA GENTL AND MARTIN HYERS
WORDS BY BRIAN FERRY

MORNING HOURS

I am not naturally a morning person, but I have become one out of necessity.

In those first hours of the day, there is stillness all around. At five o'clock, my seven-year-old is still sound asleep—and more often than not, so is my husband. So at that early hour, there's no talking, no questions, no necessary responses.

In the summer months, when there is blue sky and sunshine, it's easier to be an early bird. In those darker, grayer months of late fall and deep winter, it takes a certain resolve. It's dark out and the kitchen lights are reflected in the windows. I sit at our kitchen counter and over the next hour, I watch light come into the sky.

To begin, there is something hot. Often coffee, dark and rich, made in a Chemex and poured into my favorite mug, tempered with cream. Some mornings it is tea, nothing fancy, just PG Tips with whole milk in the same perfect mug. I like the way it fits into my hand, just so. I like the first sip, radiating warmth, a welcomed morning greeting.

I am not naturally a morning person, but I have become one out of necessity. Once we wake Liam at a quarter past six, the morning is a jumble of bathroom time, breakfast eating, lunch making, homework gathering, and then—*quick!*—out the door to school. I dislike that panicky feeling of being rushed, as well as of being late, so those first quiet hours of solitude are essential. After those hushed hours of daybreak, the possibilities are bright. Everything can unfurl from there into the very best kind of day—one full of inspiration and work in the studio, drawn to a close with a home-cooked meal shared with my family.

Lynn Russell is the letterpress printer and designer for Satsuma Press. She works and makes her home in Corvallis, Oregon with her husband, Ben, and their seven-year-old son, Liam. Liam has a rare neuromuscular disorder called Spinal Muscular Atrophy Type 2. He is, of course, much more than his diagnosis—charming, smart, mischievous. Many things are altogether different than what they ever could have imagined—sometimes heartbreaking, sometimes amazing, and sometimes both at the same time.

PHOTOGRAPH BY JILLIAN GUYETTE
WORDS BY LYNN RUSSELL

ENTERTAINING DETAILS

PHOTOGRAPH ESSAY BY ANDREA GENTL AND MARTIN HYERS

The simple intricacies that surface naturally in our preparations for company provide
an unimposing uniqueness to our gatherings. The way the cloth napkins twist upward on a solitary corner,
for example, or the bow of the apron ties and parcel strings. Appreciating these organic
occurrences magnifies the beauty of the unplanned, and eliminates an
all-too-common air of superficiality. It's time to enjoy the details of entertaining.

DRINKING CHOCOLATE

Three small cups of the thick drinking chocolate are brought
to our table, con panna—*with cream.*

Soaked from the rain, I open the front door to the tiny apartment in Italy—my temporary home. I lean out the window; the late November light is a cool blue, dotted with the amber glow of shops awakening for business after siesta. Across the street, the owner of a chocolate lounge rolls up the metal gate, opens the front door, and spills jazz onto the street. I see two new friends wave to me, and I run downstairs to meet them for hot chocolate—*cioccalata calda.*

We gather around a small wooden table and begin talking in English and in Italian. Three small cups of the thick drinking chocolate are brought to our table, *con panna*—with cream. Mine is *al peperoncino*, and the warm bittersweetness is followed by the heat of the pepper. More people filter in from the street, and each time the door opens a gust of cool air sneaks in, but I feel as though a warm blanket covers me

After leaving Italy, on a wintry, snowed-in day, my friends and I put on some music and work with what we have—chocolate pudding. We heat it in a saucepan and it almost resembles the same spoon-coating drink we had in Italy. Since then, I've found that some good chocolate, milk, cornstarch, and creativity—sea salt, lavender, maybe some pistachio—do the trick. I crave this dessert—not just the indulgence itself but the experience of consuming it, the slowing down, the savoring.

PHOTOGRAPH AND WORDS BY KRISTIN TEIG

MEN BEHIND THE MEAL

INTERVIEWS AND PHOTOGRAPHS BY ANAIS WADE AND DAX HENRY

Three artists dedicate their lives to the dishes and meat cuts that keep their patrons smiling. Journalists and photographers Anais and Dax sit down with these culinary creatives, each of whom do their work thoughtfully, and love to see friends, family, and guests enjoying a dish together around the table.

INAKI AIZPITARTE

Meet Inaki, poet of the palate and the plate. A fixed menu that changes every day with the rhythm of seasons and inspiration, his plates are an unforgettable sensorial experience. Inaki was born and raised in the South West of France, in the Basque Country, a region that still inspires his cuisine. Former apprentice of the fresh and local produce obsessed Alain Passard, the young Aizpitarte makes high-end French gastronomy affordable and innovative. We still dream of his duck fat bouillon with licorice and tarragon, or his marrow served like a slice of butter with radishes "French style" sprinkled with seaweed.

What did you eat for breakfast this morning?
Hmm, nothing. I didn't feel well. But usually I have a hot chocolate with milk, and then I switch to coffee. I rarely eat in the morning, sometimes a shortbread cookie or "petit sable."

An ingredient that puts you in a good mood.
There are ten million ingredients that make me happy, especially when they're incredibly fresh and of exceptional quality. The ingredient of the day: arroche, from the family of spinach.

If you could only save one thing from your kitchen, what would it be?
My sous-chef!

When did you know that you had made it, that it was going to be your life?
I was always attracted to the idea of cooking, but I had never done anything about it. I discovered professional kitchens while traveling, when I was in need to make some money. I was a dishwasher in a restaurant in Israel around twelve years ago, while I was hoping I would get a job as gardener somewhere else. I ended up being a kitchen helper instead. When I sent my first plate out, I knew it was going to be my life. It was a great Mediterranean restaurant, that mixed French and

Italian and pretty much did "author gastronomy". It immediately clicked for me, and I knew that the moment I would set a foot back in France, I would train to become a chef.

A controversial ingredient.
Tuna right now. But also all the ingredients that travel too much, that we overuse, that get shipped for random reasons not in season. The tuna from Saint-Jean-de-Luz is subjected to quotas, but I can't help but eat some, within the quotas, of course! It's a childhood taste.

What is your relationship to farmers and small producers?
It is the core of our work. We pay great attention to it. I love our relationships with the produce sellers, the people who find the best fish for us, the butchers, the ones who make olive oil, the others who hunt down spices, etc. We meet a lot of interesting people.

Do you shop yourself for the restaurant or do you have buyers that help you find the perfect ingredients?
There are several networks in between restaurants, which allow us to obtain beautiful ingredients. But then there are little things that we hunt down ourselves here and there.

PHOTOGRAPH BY ANAIS WADE AND DAX HENRY

GREGORY MARCHAND

The best techniques from both sides of the Atlantic, based on local and fresh ingredients—that's what Gregory Marchand will feed you at Frenchie. "Less is more" is the motto, even though we cannot help being marveled by the beautiful composition of each plate, punctuated with colorful and unique ingredients. We arrived before the restaurant opened, and found his expecting wife and son hanging out with some friends at the outdoor bistro tables, a perfect welcoming committee. There is a fixed menu that changes with the seasons; you will not regret being told what to eat. Each plate was just a little slice of heaven for our palate. From the foie gras with drunken cherries to the smoked mackerel with spring asparagus, everything was amazing. Just talking about it makes us want to hop on a flight to Paris for dinner!

One word that describes you.
Ha, it's hard to describe oneself! Happy!

Do you have a notebook in which you write your ideas?
Yes, since the very beginning when I started my project. I always had little notebooks wherever I went. I'm the kind of person who does a lot of to-do lists, who needs to write down things to remember them, to get organized. It's a whole series of lists, lists, more lists, clipboards, notebooks; I'm always a pen in hand. Very important!

Do you get suddenly woken up at night by new ideas?
It happens, but more during certain times. When I was about to open Frenchie, it was occupying 100% of my thoughts! After that I tried to take a bit of distance, even though it's only been two years.

Your three key ingredients.
Acidity is important, so lemon and vinegars. Olive oil. It's hard to choose! For this spring season the ingredient is the asparagus, but there's also morel mushrooms. There's so many! It all depends on the season.

If you weren't a chef, what would you be?
I don't know! I actually have no idea where I would be, I would probably be bored to death. I started when I was sixteen, so it is hard for me to see myself doing anything else. Like many others as a kid I wanted to be a veterinarian. I never really wanted to be a chef, it was kind of a safety net, a way to survive. At age 16 in France you have to choose your school orientation, so I chose gastronomy because I somehow liked cooking.

Who are the people who inspired you?
The first chefs I worked with in London like David Nichols from the Mandarin Oriental. Then I went to the Savoy with Simon Scott, who's now in the South of France. All the people I worked with guided me, but it took me some time to realize what I was doing, at first it was only a way to pay for rent.

Is cooking for you a political act in the current state of the world?
Yes, I think that you need to pay attention to what you buy, where you buy and when you buy it. You can already make a difference by buying while respecting the seasons, as well as locally when you can. I have some great foragers that will look for ingredients from the region. At first it was hard for me to find things in and around Paris, because I had lived abroad for ten years; it takes time to find the right people. Now I have a good little network that allows me to have more ethical ingredients in my plate.

What are your strongest memories of your experience abroad?
There are several, but mostly the discovery of a gastronomy through its culture. In London I loved working for Jamie Oliver, making "Italian-Brit" food, it really liberated me to work there, to forget all the rigid rules that are being taught to you in cooking school. In the United States I worked for the Gramercy Tavern in New York City, where they were all about farm-to-table. It is really interesting to work in kitchens that get their inspiration from all around the world, in cosmopolitan cities like London and New York, it opens up your horizons.

PHOTOGRAPH BY ANAIS WADE AND DAX HENRY

HUGO DESNOYER

We met Hugo on a cold and rainy Wednesday morning in June. He apologized for being late, since a couple of clients had held him up. We went to the café next door to interview him and warm up a little. He has a friendly but sure face, and he talked to us about his passion for what he calls a "noble material" while he sipped on his watered-down espresso and smoked cigarettes. The man known for being the president's butcher was just a good guy you could strike up a conversation with in a bistro. Bon vivant and food lover, Desnoyer understands the challenges that meat producers, cattle ranchers, and butchers face in an era of industrialization and endless search for profit, to the detriment of the environment and health of millions of us.

What's a typical day like at the butcher shop for you?
We start pretty early in the morning. One of my guys starts at 2:45 a.m. to go to the Rungis Market, because there's always something we need to get to complete our inventory on a daily basis, like veal liver, or rabbit. Everyone else arrives at the shop around 5 a.m. We start by taking all the orders from the restaurants, and there's quite a lot. Around 6 a.m. two of my guys start laying out the shop window and display, because it is redone every day. The manager then starts taking care of orders from private clients. At 6:45 a.m. the delivery guy arrives and we load his van. The first customers come in the shop around 7:30 or 8 a.m. And then the day goes on.

What are your criteria when you choose a cow?
I mainly buy Limousine cows. They should be anywhere from four to six years old. They should have had at least two or three babies, which gives them a great morphology; the intra-muscular grain becomes finer, and the meat becomes more marbled and tasty. The most important thing is what the cows eat. There are certain things that I won't allow them to eat: silage for example is catastrophic—even if the cow is a great one, it will be incredibly watery. But crushed or ground corn is good, mixed with wheat or even alfalfa, which is full of iron and gives a nice ruby tone to the meat. Toward the end it's also good if the cows are fed beets, potatoes, and linseed meal, which is costly but so good for the meat's fat. The bones should be fine, the tail lively and fat.

What was your dream job as a kid?
I had no clue what I wanted to do. I wasn't a good student in high school. My father quickly understood that school wasn't for me, so he made me do little jobs in car shops, as a waiter, but nothing ever really worked for me. But the day that he sent me to work in a butcher shop when I was fifteen, it clicked. I was lucky enough to work with great people.

What are the three qualities that you seek in a piece of meat?
The color, the marbling and the aging. On a piece of sirloin or rib-eye the red should be deep, purple-red, garnet-colored, and ideally marbled. Meat should always be aged. Here in our shop we age the meat for four weeks. Three weeks in a fridge at the slaughter house, with all the fat still around the meat for better conservation. After three weeks the animal is cut in 4 pieces and sent to my shop. The natural enzyme during that process will break down the small nerve fibers, which will make the meat more tender and tasty. Meat maturation is unfortunately a practice that is being lost today; after four weeks, the meat looses 20% of its muscular weight, which means less meat to sell and less profit.

What's your favorite meal?
I'm simple kind of guy. A good terrine with a piece of bread. Or seared blood sausage with a good salad. Salt, pepper and butter with a good meat.

Your first memory of food?
As a kid my family didn't have much money. On weekends we'd often visit my grandmother who raised chickens, rabbits and would sometimes buy beef. I would help my grandmother kill the rabbit, and I loved cooking with her.
But my best memory of meat goes back to when I was twenty years old when I found a beautiful fat and marbled piece of meat from Normandy. I shared it with a friend on a Sunday. The fat is what made the taste!

PHOTOGRAPH BY ANAIS WADE AND DAX HENRY

COOKING ALONE

Food might be the most social of those pursuits, but it is that time alone that allows us to develop an intimacy with our subject.

So many creative pursuits demand a period of solitude for the germination of projects—writing, music-making, painting. The same can be said of cooking. Aside from music, food might be the most social of those pursuits, but it is that time alone that allows us to develop an intimacy with our subject— here, the raw ingredients that will become a meal. Without distractions, we pay closer attention to the behavior of our materials, and gain a nuanced understanding of their qualities and how they come together to create a dish.

The long, dark hours of winter evenings and the tough, unyielding root vegetables of the season lend themselves to a kind of engaged and reflective cooking. It can't be a coincidence that in summer we practically abandon the stove, opting for simple, refreshing foods that require as little time as possible to prepare, while in winter it is soups, stews, roasts and braises that enamor us—activities that beg a little patience. Cooking brings a welcome warmth into the home, a buffer against the chill of the season.

Cutting pounds of carrots, potatoes, parsnips, or winter squash asks that the cook yield a little to the process—those tubers don't offer themselves up easily. And that's where the process becomes a hypnotic, almost trance-like activity. There is the gentle resistance of the fibrous vegetable and the slow, careful push of the knife, over and over, while a pot is filled with the contents and readied for a long simmer.

Those moments to myself, lost in the rhythms of chopping, prepping and combining, are often what I crave most from cooking, whether it's for thirty minutes, three hours or all of a Sunday. Later the house may be filled with friends and family. There's little that I love more than that ritual— spending time with the people I care about, eating together. But I relish the time prior to the meal equally, that hushed, engrossed period where I am alone with my materials.

PHOTOGRAPH BY RINNE ALLEN & LUCY ALLEN GILLIS
WORDS BY KIMBERLEY HASSELBRINK

A PICNIC IN THE FOREST

"Climb the mountains and get their good tidings.
Nature's peace will flow into you as sunshine flows into trees.
The winds will blow their own freshness into you, and the storms their energy,
while cares will drop away from you like the leaves of Autumn."

—JOHN MUIR

I love the ritual of eating outdoors, any time of year and often alone. While I sometimes feel awkward eating alone in a restaurant, it never feels this way out of doors. I feel perfectly at home sitting amongst the trees, moss, and water. Picnicking during colder months can be a little more complicated, but not by much, and I like to be ready for a spontaneous outdoor feast at any time. Here are a few tips for spur-of-the-moment, cold-weather picnics.

WINTER PICNIC ESSENTIALS Bring a small tarp to keep under your picnic blanket, a compass in case you got lost, and plenty of water.

WEAR Comfortable, waterproof shoes for exploring. Layers and a waterproof jacket in case of a change in weather. Hat, scarf, and gloves.

EAT Bring soup and drinks in thermoses, bread, fruit, nuts, and other snacks.

DO Write in a journal, press ferns, hike, climb a tree, ride a bike.

WORDS AND STYLING BY CHELSEA FUSS

PHOTOGRAPHS BY LISA WARNINGER

TWO

ENTERTAINING FOR TWO

∘ ∘

TEA FOR TWO

PHOTOGRAPHS BY ALICE GAO
STYLING BY THE JEWELS OF NEW YORK
AND ANDREW STEWART

The worn wooden table is covered in teacup rings.
Some call them stains, but I prefer to think of them as steeped memories.

Crisp fall air calls for the delicate warmth of knit sweaters and sips of tea. As the sun begins to bid *adieu* through the open windows, I nestle near the stove. The fire crackling under the kettle heats my hovering hands. Calling me close, the boiling water begins to sing as I carefully spoon Wuyi oolong tea leaves into the glass pot. I pause to soak in the sounds of my favorite season, the rustling of autumn leaves beyond the curtain.

Steamed water awakens the long, twisted oolong leaves from their deep sleep, and they begin to dance about in the pot. Even as the hustle and bustle of evening energy tries to pull me away, I stay close to the teapot. My tiny kitchen, still scented from last night's earthy squash and herbs, begins to take on a roasted aroma. Suddenly, I don't need the sweater draped on the corner of the chair.

The art of the steep comes to a close in minutes that feel like seconds. I don't bother to reset the stovetop timer that is flashing zeroes; it's my way of escaping the fleeting hours of the evening. With the tea leaves resting for a second session, I open the door to a cupboard overflowing with cups. The perfect sweet but sturdy pair are tucked in the corner. I reach through their handles, pressing my thumb into the porcelain, and warm them with a quick rinse of hot water. Placing them near the pot, I hear a gentle knock at the door and a jiggle of the handle that sends me to greet a dear friend. There is just something about sharing a steep that tugs at my heartstrings.

The worn wooden table is covered in teacup rings. Some call them stains, but I prefer to think of them as steeped memories. Gently pouring tea into the cups, we quickly steal a few sips that remind us of earthy barley and rich bites of sweet raisins. I settle into my favorite Sunday sweater, hoping that the few loose buttons can hold on for one more season. With just a cup in our hands, we head out into autumn twilight. The light peach skies seem to cast a flickering glow and whispered winds flutter through amber leaves. Steam escapes from the tea and mingles with chilled air. Embracing the cups with both palms, every earthy oolong sip roots us in the season and in the quiet moments that can only be shared by the closest of friends.

Bits and pieces of crumbled golden leaves line the sidewalk and roll over our laces. I purposefully crunch a few under my shoes just to hear the familiar sound. The air is quickly changing from crisp to cold, but we don't mind. We hold the cups closer to our hearts; tiny wisps of steam escape to play in the twilight sky as we savor the last few sips that have cooled.

Huddled back by the stove, we share a second steep and try to hold on to what's left of the evening. We casually make plans for next Sunday's tea-infused stroll, knowing that nothing would keep us from sipping under autumn twilight, not even the coolest of nights. All we need is a warmer sweater and a larger cup of tea

Words by Alexis Siemons and floral design by Ariel Dearie Flowers

THE SEASON OF
INTENTIONAL GATHERINGS

Every city has a sex and an age which have nothing to do with demography.
Rome is feminine. So is Odessa. London is a teenager, an urchin,
and in this, hasn't changed since the time of Dickens.
Paris, I believe, is a man in his twenties in love with an older woman.

—JOHN BERGER

If Berger is right and this is true, my city is a curmudgeonly old man. He talks a lot about the past. He complains. He never says thank you, and doesn't expect to be thanked. But he works hard, refusing acclaim, and once you soften him up, he treats you with incomparable warmth. On the coldest day of the year, he gets up before the sun, scrapes the ice off the windshield of his car, and drives his grandson to the skating rink for hockey practice. This is a city "chastened by an outsized landscape and extravagant weather, and chastened again by an awareness that the whole of human history has occurred elsewhere." It doesn't think too highly of itself.

For half the year, Winnipeg, Manitoba, is bitter and dark and frozen. It is as far from the ocean as a city can be—in every direction. There is only sky and land and more sky and wind. The cold is difficult to explain to someone who's never experienced it. It's numbing, somnolent, and so silent that you can hear the absence of sound. There are days where the radio warns of frostbite in seconds and hypothermia in minutes. There are weeks when you leave home for work in the dark and return home from work in the dark, never seeing daylight. The sidewalks are walled with heaps of snow and walking down them is lonely. There are no icicles because nothing melts. My Oma used to dry clean my Opa's suits by burying them in the snow, confident they would stay dry. Boiling water, thrown outdoors, turns to vapour. The only smell is the cold. If summer here swells

and sighs, winter cracks and sleeps. The most ordinary tasks turn into courageous undertakings: fetching the mail, filling the car with gas, taking the dog out. Bus drivers transform into heroes—picking up the almost frozen, but still alive, from the sides of the icy roads.

In summer, gatherings of friends are often spontaneous and imprecise. We might run into each other and spend the rest of the evening eating watermelon in someone's backyard or sharing beers at a favourite pub. There is little distinction between your house and my house, between my front porch and the boulevard. The restaurant blurs into the sidewalk; the day blurs into the night. In winter, the opposite is true: gatherings are deliberate and brave. We arrive at each other's homes wrapped in sweaters and parkas and scarves, our faces and feet aching from the immediate warmth. We peel off our mittens and place them on the stove to dry. We bring foods that restimulate our sense of smell and remind us of colour: rich red wine, baked sweet potatoes, pecan pie. We are reminded also (and perhaps more importantly) of each other. We have been isolated by the cold and eschewed the outside for days. We've turned inward. Now, together, undistracted by the sounds of the street, committed to our present time and place, locked in by wind and ice, we are enlivened by community. If we could, we'd never leave. Winter is the recognition, in the form of a season, that that we need each other.

PHOTOGRAPHS BY ANAIS WADE AND DAX HENRY
WORDS BY NIKAELA PETERS

Winter came down to our home one night
Quietly pirouetting in on silvery-toed slippers of snow,
And we, we were children once again.[1]

BILL MORGAN, JR.

WINTER'S REST

PHOTOGRAPHS BY TEC PETAJA AND STYLING BY CHELSEA PETAJA

WORDS BY ELISE YETTON

Start a new tradition, not centered on travel or shopping or working toward a new year, but focused on creating a time to enjoy the comforts of those closest to you.

In nature, the changing of seasons is significant to the life cycle. Days grow shorter, and as the light dies, so does the flora it feeds. Flowers and plants recede from the plummeting cold while once-green leaves turn to gold, then russet red, and fall to rest atop freezing soil. Birds fly to escape the onset of winter and wild beasts, with stores of food tucked away, hide beneath the ground to sleep, their hibernating dreams filled with the warmth of spring. For them, the year's end brings harsh times, but also rest and promises of a season of plenty just around the corner.

So it should be for us—humans—that the end of summer brings a time for peace, a winding down in which to gather our stores and regain our strength. But even as the golden sun diminishes and the world outside encourages us to simplify, the winter is only another season to push through for many. Too often we forget to leave our lives behind, and instead allow the worries of production and everyday-ness to seep in. The new days of spring have yet to begin, and already we make plans and lay preparations, much to our own exhaustion.

It is time to disconnect, to fill our wintry lives not with events but with rest. Start a new tradition, not centered on travel or shopping or working toward a new year, but focused on creating a time to enjoy the comforts of those closest to you. Whether with a sibling, a friend, a parent, or a lover, greet the frosty morning before the sun, no matter how much your body may plead to stay beneath the quilts. Rub the sleep from your eyes as the kettle boils. Then, with piping mug in hand, curl up on the front porch and share a quiet sunrise.

THE SCENT OF SALTED AIR

A TREATISE FOR SHARED TRAVEL

CONCEPT BY NIKOLE HERRIOTT AND TARA O'BRADY

PHOTOGRAPHS BY MICHAEL GRAYDON

In distance covered, within the click of the kilometres progressed,
there is bond forged in the companionship of travel. It is a different sort of connection.
With the separation from home that other becomes our anchor; that person brings along
our notion of home. They keep it nearby.

Michael and Nikole packed a car and drove the 1300 kilometres between the Canadian provinces of Ontario and Prince Edward Island, to a town they had never been to before. For seven days in the midst of autumn, a 150-year-old farmhouse at the edge of the ocean was their home.

The trip was the first of what is to become an annual pilgrimage.

There is a charm in imagining experiences tied at ends to those with whom they are shared. That its record held between the two — both essential in their contribution.

In distance covered, within the click of the kilometres progressed, there is bond forged in the companionship of travel. It is a different sort of connection. With the separation from home that other becomes our anchor; that person brings along our notion of home. They keep it nearby.

While our world opens up with size and possibility, it simultaneously condenses into the company of another, as our everyday usual falls away. Within that company, the unknown becomes familiar in partnership, through days spent specifically in tandem.

In this case, we're speaking of memories of days spent on the tip of an island. Looking through windowpanes effervescent with bubbles trapped in the glass. Meals shared, and chairs pulled close to the table and to each other. Walks on soft sand after a feast of clams with butter and beer, to return the shells to the waters from whence they came. The taste of potatoes dug from red earth, the likes of which you won't find anywhere else. The act of battening down the hatches and together bundling up against a storm, with winds that wailed against ancient walls in exhilarating gusts.

Clothes brought in from drying, branded with the scent of salted air.

This particular trip was only the beginning, setting a the foundation for all that is yet to come.

Tradition is, at its most basic, habit invested with importance. There are routines, movements in which we've infused the conviction that they have value. To step into the same shoes and follow the same footsteps to the same destinations, and each time we are rewarded in how the journey differs. In how the light changes and how tart the plums were that one year, wild and tiny. In the crinkles of a paper map that will grow soft, like fabric, as they are folded over and over again.

Travel amplifies the effect, one often at best advantage when there is another to appreciate it. Every adventure, as we are aware of its boundary and precious transience, contributing to the whole of a collaborative history.

IN THE MORNING A stack of hot buttermilk waffles with proper maple syrup, bowls of vanilla bean oats, as you like them.

AT MIDDAY East coast seafood chowder and tender biscuits, mussels steamed in wine with pan-fried brioche for dipping.

IN THE EVENINGS The simplest clams, salted butter and our definitive fries, pan roasted steak with root vegetables.

FOR SWEETS Sugared port plums in pâte brisée, sticky toffee puddings with a pour of bourbon caramel.

View these recipes at www.kinfolkmag.com/recipes.

PRODUCTION BY NIKOLE HERRIOTT
WORDS BY TARA O'BRADY

FEW

ENTERTAINING FOR A FEW

○ ○ ○

HONEY HARVEST

PHOTOGRAPHS BY LEO PATRONE AND WORDS BY SARAH WINWARD

FILM BY TIGER IN A JAR

One day, the desire to be a beekeeper came over me. The next thing I knew, I had purchased some bees and loaded them into my car. I could hear them buzzing in the backseat as I drove home. The sound fluctuated, becoming louder and more feverish when I drove over bumps, and I wondered what I had gotten myself into.

It took time for me to become acquainted with the bees, but after a few weeks we were friends. Now I have 10,000 friends living in my backyard. At first I would walk out and look at them from afar, but soon I was picking ripe tomatoes from my garden, barefoot, right next to their hive. As I became more comfortable around them I would sit close and watch their flight path; my bees fly out southeast from their hive, with a stop at the Russian sage and trumpet vine on their way toward the mountains. In the morning there is a constant, perfectly timed stream. As one's feet leave the landing dock, another one flies in. As soon as he is in, the next one is taking off the edge of the dock. It is perfectly coordinated, like clockwork.

When they come back to the hive from a day's work of dancing with the flowers, the dusty pollen on their feet is in globs of all different colors and shapes. One day I was able to see what bee keepers call the waggle dance, the curious dance where a bee flies in a figure eight with varying speeds and circumferences to let the other bees know where the good nectars are. As soon as he was done dancing, an army of bees blasted out of the entrance and headed to the prized flower. I imagine something spectacular was blooming that day that just could not be missed. As a florist, I share the sense of urgency the bees have to use a flower when it's at its peak. Watching the bees in the afternoon has become an inspirational and therapeutic break for me during a day's work. I get out of my house into the bright sunlight to visit them, and I am amazed by their constant movement. What looks like chaos from afar is intentional and well choreographed up close.

Something that is perhaps even more fascinating than watching the bees' flight pattern is studying their honeycomb. I am constantly awed by how engineered, mathematical, and precise their comb is. Each hexagonal cell is perfectly angled into the next. The wax is the color of butter and the honey inside is a perfect golden toffee.

My first taste of honey from the bees was surreal.

It is an interesting experience to taste your surroundings. With each season and each harvest, our honey has had a different color and taste; we save one bottle from each harvest and call it our special reserve. The earlier in the year we harvest, the lighter the color and the more floral the taste. The closer to autumn that we harvest, the thicker and more amber in color the honey is. Last fall we had a blooming ivy bush that the bees loved—you could hear the bush buzzing when walking past. The honey from that harvest tasted woodsy and deep, just like you would imagine honey flavored from ivy to taste.

Last summer our bees gave us honey that was lighter than ever and tasted of roses; I think it is the perfect honey. While I want to keep all the bottles of it lined up in rows in my pantry forever, I also want to give it to everyone I know. I only give jars of honey to people that I know will appreciate them. Some go to family, the closest of friends; some to complete strangers, or sprinkler repairmen that show interest. It is such a warmly received gift. People really treasure their gifts of honey. Each person I give it to, whether a close friend or the sprinkler repairman, cradles the jar in their hands when I give it to them. They hold it close to their bodies, almost hugging it. It's a wonderful thing to receive a gift that is the product of an entire summer's work. The elements used to create it came from the nectar of countless flowers and was a collaboration of 10,000 bees' time and energy. The honey in one harvest actually took longer to create than most of the bees in the hive live.

I find it satisfying to drizzle honey from my own bees over yogurt in the morning. Toast with honey just tastes better when I can look out over my garden while eating it and know that it is, in a way, the finished product of my entire garden. I am proud of the honey I give as gifts or use in my cooking, but I know that I did not make it. I merely bottle it to make consumption more convenient. It is a strange thing to be so graciously thanked for something I didn't make. I don't "keep" bees—they keep themselves, and I steal their honey; that is what beekeeping is. I have a collection of bee stings that are battle scars from foolish moves I have made while tending to the bees and not wearing protective clothing—but they are a small price to pay for an entire pantry full of liquid gold.

WHY I COOK

PHOTOGRAPHS BY HILDA GRAHNAT

WORDS BY SARAH BRITTON

I grew up having dinner with my family almost every night. Although my parents were not the most enthusiastic cooks, they made us food because it meant we could all sit together, eat, and connect as a family. It has taken me some years to understand the impact this has had on me, but now I realize how close we are because of those countless hours around the table. It has become a priority of mine to continue that tradition because I see how the meals shaped my appreciation of food, of cooking, and of family togetherness.

Even after a full day of cooking in one of my restaurants, I enjoy preparing dinner with my husband when I get home. Cooking and eating together feels so grounding. To create something beautiful together, to share nourishment, is fulfilling on levels that go far beyond fueling the body.

I am honored to be a chef; preparing and serving food to others is a primal act of nurturing. I see my work as very sacred and I approach it with a great deal of respect, because ultimately, food is love. When I look out over a packed restaurant and see guests eating meals I have prepared, I feel overwhelmingly satisfied. I know that they will leave totally nourished and excited at having discovered that healthy food can taste amazing.

A great deal of my cooking inspiration comes from following the seasons. Food is the most intimate connection we have with our earth. I make a point of eating what is seasonal and local because these foods support my personal health by preparing my body for the climate, and support the health of the environment, since foods travel shorter distances. It is not a coincidence that certain foods give us what we need during their natural growing season —high-water-content foods like cucumbers and tomatoes cool us down in the summer, while starchy, calorie-dense foods like pumpkins and beets fuel us through the winter. Seasons have a flavour if we tune into them through the gifts of each cycle; for me, spring tastes like wild leek pesto, and autumn tastes like fig and walnut jam. By taking our cues from nature, we align ourselves with the rhythms of the earth—and consequently our bodies' needs—the result of which can only be complete, natural balance and wellness.

My blog, My New Roots, began as a way to share what I had learned about wellness and healing from my Holistic Nutrition education, but it has become so much more. Over the last four years, I began sharing vegetarian, whole food recipes on My New Roots, and as more people visited my site for both the information and the recipes, a community of people that are passionate about cooking was born. There are so many people out there who are hungering for direction and guidance when it comes to preparing nutritious food, and providing that help, even to a small number, is gratifying to me. As emails from readers flow in every day praising the results of the raw brownies or the sweet potato hummus they made at home, I am called to the cutting board to produce yet another dish to satisfy those who want to take charge of their health and reclaim their kitchens. Their inspiration becomes mine, and the cycle continues. Even though we've probably never met, I can feel us standing side by side at our stovetops, making so much more than dinner.

We live in a hectic, traffic-jammed, competitive society. So often we sacrifice traditions based on preparing and eating real food for the convenience of drive-throughs and freezer dinners, convinced that by saving time in the kitchen, we'll get ahead in some other way. My mission is to encourage people to slow down and experience the simple joys of cooking, and to focus on nourishing our bodies and spirits. Through my work at the restaurants, my blog, and my daily life, I am trying to show how we can make huge changes in our lives just by making small changes in the kitchen every day. I am certain that conversation, communion, and connection will work its way back into our homes, feeding the hunger of the soul above all else.

Sarah Britton is a holistic nutritionist, vegetarian chef, and the creator of the award-winning blog My New Roots. Sarah is currently a chef at two organic restaurants in Copenhagen, Denmark, where she has earned praise for her creative and adventurous recipes.

Whenever we cook for others, we are making a statement to them.
If what we prepare and present to our family and guests is attractive, tasty, and health-supporting, we are
saying that we want them to be well and happy, to feel nurtured and strengthened.
When we offer cuisine that is made of whole and natural ingredients, we are saying that we want them to
have all the energy they need in order to make every aspect of their lives richer.
We are saying we honor them.[3]

JOHN ROBBINS, MAY ALL BE FED

PRESERVING SUMMER

*During the doldrums of winter, a jar of peach preserves can bring warmth
to rival any steaming bowl of soup.*

Peaches come at the sunset of summer, which may be why the hues of a dying sun are emblazoned on their fuzzy exteriors. They are a fruit I can't wait to eat, not even long enough to grab a napkin to catch the juices dribbling down my hands and into the crooks of my arms. In this sticky state I feel like I am in some sort of fruit-induced nirvana. The window of time for what I deem perfect peaches lasts for only a few weeks, and I can become rather frantic at the idea that this fruit's life span is so fleeting. The only solace I get is the yearly ritual of making peach preserves. Canning has the power of transforming food into something that smacks of the immortal—until, of course, I get a hankering for bottled summer and pop the seal. During the doldrums of winter, a jar of peach preserves can bring warmth to rival any steaming bowl of soup.

My mom has a peach tree in her yard that goes unnoticed for most of the summer, until miraculously its branches start reaching lower as they become laden with Lemon Elberta, our favorite variety of peaches. We gather boxes full of these peaches—just before they are tempted to drop off their branches—and hurry them to my grandparents' kitchen. We have canned in this cheery yellow space for as long as I can remember, and I know its history with canning goes back even further. We bring up all the necessary tools from the basement: boxes of empty bottles, kettles, blanchers, funnels, jar lifters, and paper sacks filled with tinging metal rings. The familiar hum of the process starts as pots are filled with water, the rolling cadence of boiling begins, and ripe peaches are submerged and blanched. We talk as we work, our knives keeping metronome-like time with the sticky business of cutting away fuzz from flesh. After a few hours of this work—cutting, heating, stirring, pouring, and finally a boiling hot water bath—we are left with amber-colored jars of peaches in a new form. Glass instead of skin. Immortality instead of impending brown flesh. I instantly feel much more at ease with my beloved fruit.

Now, as winter casts blue shadows in the kitchen, I unscrew the metal ring on the jar and anticipate the smell that will escape the sealed lid. Of course, it is missing its former cohorts of heavily steamed air and pink-flushed cheeks, but otherwise it is just as though I have inhaled deeply while stirring my peach and sugar concoction on the stove. In this way I find the act of canning to be an experience we don't often get with our food. To have spent time with it before opening the jar makes it feel more like we are meeting up with an old friend, rather than a blind date. (A relationship that we unfortunately we have all too often with our food.) If we are lucky, we may have even brought the peaches to life starting with a seed and some dark soil, which of course means the result counts us as the dearest of friends.

Along with this deep-rooted relationship, this jar of preserves has one more offering: it brings back the warmth of a late-summer day with its unbelievable amounts of peaches, of stickiness that drips, and of conversations that muse over the dying summer and excitedly plot about the impending fall. A day that included bottling peaches also got bottled itself, in a way. As I sit alone at the table, my toast heaped with golden jam, I can almost feel the apron strings tugging at my neck. My mom's voice is as audible as my crunchy bites, and the crooks of my arms feel tickled by a sweet sticky juice. Summer couldn't feel closer, although it is months away.

PHOTOGRAPH BY NIKOLE HERRIOTT
WORDS BY JULIE WALKER

OREGON COAST

PHOTOGRAPH ESSAY BY LAURA D'ART AND ANDY PIPE

DRIVE

DUTCH OVEN BREAD

PHOTOGRAPH BY ANAIS WADE AND DAX HENRY
VIEW FILM AT WWW.KINFOLKMAG.COM/FILMS
FILM BY TIGER IN A JAR

WANDERERS AT THE TABLE

PHOTOGRAPHS BY WILLIAM HEREFORD

WORDS BY REBECCA PARKER

The first frost has come early this year, and with it the simultaneous closing of doors and shutting of windows, an echo of a common pursuit of warmth. We enter a period of physical and emotional darkness; we are left to burrow in our homes, yet we need connection more than we do in any other season. Winter demands action, necessitates movement; an axe slices through wood, chili bubbles on the stovetop. If we sit motionless in the harsh months of winter, we wither. We must endeavor to find our comfort again. We must chop wood to build fires, we must slice hearty potatoes for soups, and we must choose to pursue our community of friends, lest we freeze out here, in the stinging winds of the darkest nights, where porches are abandoned and streetlights cast shadows on empty streets.

Friends arrive; a few knock, but most ignore this pedantic ritual and walk through the back door. Every other Tuesday is the same for us: a community dinner. There is pouring of wine, shuffling of feet, crowding of bodies in a small steamy kitchen. There is a communal prayer with hands in hands and heads bowed. There is scooping, sharing, and passing over a long table spilling with food and drinks and lanky arms. There are forks waving in emphatic conversations, and there are ears pulled low to hear our neighbors.

Around the table, strings connect our hearts—tugging and pulling and lifting. Some of us are parents, some single. Some are lonely, some secure. Some are solemn, some garrulous. Sometimes there are five of us; other nights, fifteen. Regardless, all come for community.

The famous agrarian author Wendell Berry claimed that he wasn't anti-technology—he was just pro-community. And we, as a group, are not anti-culture, nor anti-technology—we just believe that community takes sacrifice and purpose. For us, community takes a committed meal together every other week. It takes coordinating the wine pick-up and the sweet dessert creations. It takes

the meal planning and abundant hospitality of one family opening their doors to us. It takes a guided and intentional discussion about the deep and wide travails and joys of our daily—occasionally mundane, occasionally novel—lives.

The alternative, we have discovered, is just wandering. Before the dinners started, we floated amongst each other in similar, occasionally concentric circles, without much more than a transient overlap. This nomadic, grazing existence, while diverting, bore no forward movement. Many of us felt busy without purpose, others felt bored, and most all of us felt unabashedly lonely. But from our spinning and our hurtling, we recognized the need for community as we recognized the need for oxygen and nature and art. And we now understand with the deep weight of our planted souls that community is not a drift. It is purposeful and it is sought after. It is sprinkled with whimsy, and it abides in a place where we can be present to one another.

Our routine community dinners are a tiny yet staunch stand against each of our years of flailing. We feel the pull of gravity back toward the earth and her lush soil, and when we come together and find the ground again, a light shines in the darkness of our winters. We are finally, finally building a fire to heat our isolated days.

Our original vision was simple: to foster a rhythm of intentional community created over sharing meals together. We are not a fancy bunch, nor are we seekers of crafting or aesthetic perfection. But our food is fresh and abundant, and our conversations are sincere. Our place settings are simple, but the welcome through the front (or back) door is deep and reverberates from the threshold.

We stand amidst the winters of life, and we build fires. We have the choppers of the wood, the stokers of the flame, and the stirrers of the chili pot. We hope you join us—or join your own friends and family—in an upheaval against wandering, and give yourself to a rebellious pursuit of community.

Dinner time at Knauer Farm with JJ Goode, Alan Systma, Nick Fauchald,
Ian Knauer, Peter Pawlick, William Hereford, and Adam Houghtaling

SUNDAY ROAST

*We meet up, either at home or in a London pub, and relive the Sunday lunches of childhood,
a ritual so strongly ingrained that the weekend would just seem wrong without it.*

CHARLOTTE BLAND It wasn't until I grew up and left home that I realized how important Sunday lunch is to the English psyche. When I was a child, it was just part of family life—on Sunday we had lunch in the dining room, my grandparents often joined us, and Mum served a great Sunday roast.

My sister and I laid the table, arranged condiments and candles (essential in the English winter gloom), and ferried sauce boats and serving spoons before the rested meat, roast potatoes, and vegetables were put on the table for the family to share.

If lunch was roast beef, there were Yorkshire puddings—very exciting since the extra batter was saved for pancakes the next day—and with roast chicken, always bread sauce, my favorite. Sometimes there was roast pork with applesauce made from the Bramleys stacked in the shed, a taste of the autumn garden in darkest winter.

There was always pudding, perhaps a crumble or tart, with steaming hot custard, or rice pudding with a crisp golden skin, and a strong cheddar with biscuits. After lunch was the walk. Either a quick march to the sea—the squally wind blowing away post-lunch sluggishness—or, if there was enough light, a more sedate ramble along the river. This came with the promise of pooh sticks from my parents to entice reluctant children, for whom it seemed "so far," before heading home at dusk to toast crumpets on the fire and read the papers.

Fast forward a few decades, and since I can't get home to Devon to share Sunday lunch with my parents very often, this weekly meal has transitioned to bring together my city family of friends. We meet up, either at home or in a London pub, and relive the Sunday lunches of childhood, a ritual so strongly ingrained that the weekend would just seem wrong without it.

BRIAN FERRY I vividly remember my first Sunday roast in London. I had just moved to London from New York City and it had been raining heavily for days. It was a raw, cold November and the days were dark and short. I spent the morning underneath a flimsy umbrella, trudging around neighborhoods and unsuccessfully looking for a flat to rent. I was fighting a peculiar loneliness, which surely must be felt by many expats after arriving in a bustling, but strange, foreign city. At dusk, I passed a warm pub on the corner. The windows were fogged over and I was greeted by laughter as I stepped inside.

That day marked the start of my love for the British tradition of Sunday roasts. There was a group of friends seated at a long table drinking wine and celebrating a birthday. In the corner, a couple had finished their roast pork and read the Sunday paper in postprandial bliss. I sat at a table near the fireplace where my soggy shoes could dry. I ordered a pint of ale and when my food arrived—roast beef, duck fat potatoes, Yorkshire pudding, and greens—I immediately relaxed and forgot about the miserable weather outside.

Since then, I have enjoyed numerous Sunday roasts in England and gathered around tables in pubs and at home with friends and family. Often we sit down and it is light outside; when we get up from the table hours later, it is dark. I love that a Sunday roast takes place in the afternoon. There, it happily occupies the largest part of your day, ensuring that the most you will manage after lunch is a nap (or perhaps a walk in the park, if you're the ambitious type).

Now that my move back to New York City is imminent, I am buying a tin for Yorkshire puddings and looking for places to buy duck fat for the roast potatoes. Forget about the brunch habit of New Yorkers—I intend to make Sunday roast a weekend tradition of my own.

PHOTOGRAPHS AND WORDS BY CHARLOTTE BLAND AND BRIAN FERRY

FORGING FAMILY

We look forward to joining our ragtag group of friends who shared an understanding—
who know what it's like to be miles away from that sense of family.

There's something rather sanctimonious about clichés that makes us want to prove them wrong. They form immediate conclusions without taking into account the different facets of our personal preferences, tastes, or personality. They assume. These assumptions are a threat to our individuality and sense of self. Yet clichés abound: *The grass is always greener on the other side. The best things come to those who wait. You don't know a good thing til it's gone.* Clichés irk us but we still repeat them.

Then you live and you grow and you come to realise the truths within that which you once dismissed as cliché.

We start out life as part of a unit, a familial nucleus of common ground. It's a boisterous rabble of growing siblings, wherein a connection is shared, freeness of speech is exerted, and an unspoken emotional responsibility is professed to one another. The house is rife with heartbeats—all resonating at a different timbre, but collectively one. A family.

Before we know it, we withdraw from that nucleus to branch out on our own. We move hundreds—sometimes thousands—of miles away to form a life alone, or in pairs if we are blessed. The cities and towns full of strangers we now call home feel separate from the familiar warmth and safety of our own nucleus. Soon, that feeling we once shared is nothing more than a pang of nostalgia.

Over time, we acquire roommates and new relationships, but it's never quite the same. It is now that we realise there is only one heartbeat in the house. Your family, that unit and all that came with it, is far away. How you wish you'd appreciated just how *good a thing* it really was when you had them, before it became nothing more than a liminal recollection.

There are emails, texts, phone calls, and maybe even the occasional card in the mail, yet it never feels the same. For all the blessings technology and modernity supply to us, they also act as cruel alienators. So we revert. We recall that which is lost—that *good thing* we need desperately in our life. A supportive community. A house full of laughter. A room full of people whose presence alone nurtures and entertains us. Acceptance. Warmth. A connection. An…ease.

The seasons cycle and winter comes. Its pallid texture weighs wearily on our psyche. Our bones echo its chill. Has it always been like this? We remember winter with our family, but it always felt warm, smelled sweet, and was welcomed. But this

I found myself in this situation one cold winter. Only my heartbeat echoed between my four walls and the sensation just felt wrong. I realised that I was not the only one. Many of my friends were born into busy family households and now, all grown up, they were living by themselves or in pairs, many miles away from relatives. Perhaps this connection we shared with our family was something that could be forged between us friends.

We came together just to be—to feel a sense of self through a sense of each other. Quickly, a routine was established and once a week, everyone spilled into my home. Guests arrived at staggered times throughout the designated evening to have their olfactory senses greeted with an aroma of whatever was bubbling on the stove for them. Shoes were kicked off and jackets hastily shoved off chilly shoulders, cast aside with the defenses often put up to protect ourselves. Friends sprawled out on the rug, the settee, the chairs, or pottered in the kitchen. There was always something needing to be put in the oven or chopped, and eager hands were ready to assist.

Gone was the harried prep that occurs when you are having people over—the rush to tuck stray magazines and newspapers under the stairs, in cupboards, and behind cushions. Informality was the order as all indiscretions were okay around family. We let our guard down.

We began to slowly understand that it's ok to laugh and be laughed at with this auspicious gathering. Egos were brushed aside and comedic one-upmanship prevailed. Mishaps and spills of drinks and selves on polished floors were met with guffaws and comforting, extended hands. Arguments over trivial matters were debated with vigor and feigned self-righteousness, and quickly dissolved by laughter or by the inevitable human encyclopedia among us who always set things straight.

We realised that the kitchen was abuzz, the living room alive, and the television faded into obscurity. The beeps and pings of mobile devices went unattended as their sounds faded with the creaks of the home's old floors and doors.

Card games stripped down barriers even further as participants shifted their focus from protecting self to game strategy, allowing true personas to shine through. Conversations flowed freely and before long, a sense of belonging to this unit arrived as secrets and innermost thoughts were shared. Together we had forged a new familial nucleus.

But the rambunctiousness always comes to a stop when food is served. Plates are filled, cutlery clinks, and everything slows down. It's funny how vulnerabilities are exposed when the focus is shifted from self. Talk becomes more honest and more personal; the words mirror the spirit of the food served. Hearty, warm dishes lead to talk of things that affect the soul: love, loss, sickness, and success.

Suddenly, the cruelty of winter is diminished. Its evenings that rushed to darkness are forgotten and the shoulder-hunching temperatures no longer felt. We look forward to joining our ragtag group of friends who shared an understanding—who know what it's like to be miles away from that sense of family.

Now there is a new timbre in my home. It manifests as a shared sensation on an intuitive level, and it is pleasantly deafening. The cliché, 'You don't know a good thing til it's gone' has now been revived through the warm association of friends. At last, there is a feeling of more than one heartbeat in the house—all resonating in harmony with one another. We are home.

PHOTOGRAPHS BY LOU MORA AND STYLING BY BASH, PLEASE
WORDS BY SAER RICHARDS

WARMTH OF THE INVERTED YEAR

If summer is a window opened wide to the breadth of life, then winter must be the gathering back in of souls to rejoin one another at a common table.

Sporadic rain had mostly cleared the streets of pedestrians, ushering them into some safe warmplace. The people who were out that night were heavily bundled and galoshed against the windand the wet. There was no snow yet; maybe by Christmas. A laughing couple rode their bicycles past me while I fumbled with a ruined map. The candy-colored architecture of the old town stoodancient and asymmetrical all around me—like a stage for a crooked fairy tale, a lost scene fromDickens. On a nearby balcony a cigarette glowed red through the rising night fog. Though barely seven o'clock, it felt much later. It had been dark for hours.

The street was empty—misty wet and motionless except for me—and, for a moment, I felt like the stranger I was. I breathed into my hands and scanned the buildings for an address, a house number, anything. I was half sure this was the right street: Kongens-something-or-other. It had better be right or I'd be more than just turned around—I'd be lost. Down here the city was irregular at best, a medieval patchwork sewn together by a million alleys and waterways. What had Jacob said? "Look for the green door and the candles on the steps."

The candles on the steps. Of course…why wouldn't there be candles on the steps…out here in the rain…in Denmark?

After a few false starts, wrong turns, and double backs I finally came to it. I locked my old blue bike to an iron fence with the others. There were, indeed, candles on the steps, their small flames fighting against the mist. Wood smoke rose from the chimney above the house with the green door. From a ground floor window an orange glow spilled into the gloomy street below. Standing on my tiptoes I could see the tops of my friends inside, gathered closely around something. A game? A story? A table of food? Each of the faces through the window was dimly but warmly lit. Smiling. Talking with their hands. A bolt of laughter, audible even outside. A raised glass of wine, then Jacob at the window, waving me in. But I didn't need the formality of an invitation. The glow from the window, the ruddy countenances, the echo of laughter, the promise of mulled wine, the green door, and the candle-lit stairs were all the invitation I needed. Something was already ushering me into that safe warm place—past the candles, out of the cold, and into the light of the best of human defenses against the darkness.

I moved to Denmark in the summertime. When the days are long and the light is plentiful. Where, for a season, the warm sun draws people out from under their roofs and into broad open spaces. Into the high brightness. In the months before the long dark returns.

Copenhagen was magic that summer. Eighteen hours of light can do strange things to the mind and body—especially in a city as vibrant and colorful as the Danish capital. Parades of men and women wore subtle sunburns and subtler smiles as they cycled through the crooked city streets. Offices and shops closed for weeks to air out their staff. Grown people on lunch breaks publicly shed their clothes to soak up sun before returning to the bank and the bakery. Busy boats filled the city's waterways. Commuters lingered on their walks home, visiting long with friends at patio bars and stopping for ice cream along the canals. Apartments and homes nightly emptied their residents into courtyards and gardens for endless dinners.

That summer I often went to bed out of a

sense of duty rather than a desire to sleep, while the sky was still bright enough to keep me awake. The Scandinavian summer is something of a revolution—a throwing off of routine, and rigidity, and the confinement of walls. Each day a holiday, a celebration of light.

And then September came. The sun grew bashful. No more dinners in the garden. Autumn was a brief moment between extremes. The summer gold faded into gray by October, to wet gray by November, and then into cold wet gray by December. When the days were short; when the light was missing. The contrast between summer and winter was profound—almost painful. As an American from the Midwest I knew cold winters, but not this deep darkness. Some days—near the solstice—if it was fully overcast there might only be a few hours of useful daylight.

The long winter months are hard, arriving like an uninvited guest. Northern people have always known this. The combination of dreary weather and darkness is a recipe for despair. The season seems to offer only limitations. How then do the Danes manage the harshness of winter after winter, year after year? What inner lamp burns bright enough (individually and collectively) to keep people warm against the bleak midwinter? Against the darkness?

I didn't find my answer until I looked through the window of that house with the green door. The friends framed inside—a moving picture of good cheer—gathered together around the common things that combat the dark nights of the year as well as the dark nights of the soul: comfort food and camaraderie, wooly blankets, and bottles of wine.

The Danes have a word for this shared warmth. It's a word we do not have in English: hygge (hoo-gah). It means something like cozy and safe and peaceful and thoughtful and altogether beautiful. Hygge smells like cinnamon and feels like a child's Christmas. Maybe hygge is untranslatable because, like all the best moments in life, it can't be captured by mere words. Whether you're trying to describe young love or Holy Communion or the first moments of fatherhood, simple words are like ill-fitting clothes: small and unflattering. And while hygge can happen in any season or place, it is certainly most fully realized in the darkest moments of the year, when candles and hearth fire and twinkling bulbs and kindness are the best we have to push back the gloom. If summer is a window opened wide to the breadth of life, then winter must be the gathering back in of souls to rejoin one another at a common table. The winter draws us into our cottages and cabins and huddles us around pots of brewing cider. Winter is a collector of close comforts. The Englishman Thomas Cowper understood this unique quality of winter when he wrote, "O Winter! ruler of the inverted year...I crown thee king of intimate delights, fireside enjoyments, home-born happiness, and all the comforts that the lowly roof of undisturbed retirement, and the hours of long uninterrupted evening, know."

And that is, precisely, what I found inside the room atop the stairs with the candles—comfort, delight, and happiness. In the presence of friends I found warmth against both the cold dark of winter and the shared hardships of daily life. That night, the room with the glowing window became a sanctuary whose green door kept back the bleak weather and the black of night. Inside we were a handful of radiant souls pouring light out into the dark winter street. We were hopeful characters in a high northern story, sharing the unselfish light of hospitality and laughter and hope which are, and have always been, the great shield and sword against the melancholy shadow of the inverted year.

PHOTOGRAPHS BY TIM ROBISON
WORDS BY AUSTIN M. SAILSBURY

VINEGAR HILL HOUSE
A GOOD PLACE TO GATHER

I was exhausted. It had been one of those crazy New York days spent running way too many errands—carrying heavy bags, darting in and out of traffic, waiting in line after line. Come seven o'clock, I was ready to put it all behind me and relax; I was meeting a friend for dinner and drinks.

It was a cool, crisp night. I could see the restaurant's golden glow and I started to feel the warmth inside as I approached. When I opened the screen door and stepped into Vinegar Hill House, I was immediately transported. All thoughts of my crazy day and the bustling city across the river disappeared.

A few years ago, when Jean Adamson's landlord told her about an old carriage house available for rent in Vinegar Hill, Brooklyn, she checked it out on a whim. She immediately fell in love with the tiny neighborhood a bit off the beaten path, located off the East River waterfront just west of the Brooklyn Navy Yard. She also fell in love with the house itself and was intrigued by the unoccupied space in front of it. As she waited the year it would take to finish the renovations to the carriage house, Jean thought more about that small space. She was an accomplished chef and had often talked with her boyfriend about the possibility of opening up a restaurant. She asked the landlord if he would also be willing to rent out the empty space in front of the house for a little neighborhood gathering spot, and Vinegar Hill House was born.

Jean, along with her boyfriend Sam Buffa, opened for business three years ago. Sam is co-owner of the very stylish F.S.C. Barber shops, and you can see his influence in the restaurant's design. Sam bought reclaimed wood and bleacher boards to create banquettes and tables, and combined these rustic wood elements with potted cacti, vintage wallpaper, and interesting items collected from travels and flea markets. The wood-burning oven at the end of the open kitchen, the lit candles and vases of fresh seasonal flowers on each table, and the cozy den downstairs (complete with a fireplace) add to the feel of a modern cabin in the woods. Sam's focus on the details, both large and small, created the homey, inviting atmosphere now admired by all who visit Vinegar Hill House, and the restaurant has quickly become a destination and a home away from home.

And as for the food, it is what you would hope for, and more—it's comfort with a twist. Chef Brian Leth updates a menu of familiar dishes with his own spin, using seasonal ingredients based on the best items the purveyors are carrying each week. The food is uncomplicated, beautiful, and delicious. A sardine on toast with anchovy mayonnaise? Yes, please.

Vinegar Hill House is a refuge for New Yorkers who want a break from cooking, but still wants to feel as if they are eating in someone's home.

Vinegar Hill House is located in Brooklyn, New York. For more information and directions visit www.vinegarhillhouse.com

PHOTOGRAPHS AND WORDS BY JENNIFER CAUSEY

BEFORE COMPANY

Tonight, it's time to gather friends yet again.

I love fall. I look better in pants and sweaters than in shorts and t-shirts. I prefer hot soup to gazpacho, and the bounty of fresh food available seems endless at harvest time. We cling to the last remnants of summer and host guests as often as we can before receding into quiet hibernation for winter. Tonight, it's time to gather friends yet again.

Whether it's a simple affair or a full-on dinner party, I prefer planning to last-minute scrambling. It's through this preparation that I take comfort in my time alone. I make a list of things to do either days or hours before, jotting notes in my little book, organizing my needs according to location in the market. I think apples seem timely, perhaps a crumble or a crisp. But as I wander the narrow aisles of my favourite produce stall, I reject that notion. Quietly considering, firmly grasping a piece of fruit, my mind calmly racing—the plan in my book begins to change. As the last of the season's plums come into view, I know it must be: this time we'll host our nearest and dearest with

pie. Tart and fluid, biting the backs of our cheeks. Plum pie.

My quiet plotting continues as I unpack my paper bags. Fruit and flour, a fresh bag of sugar, and cold butter. As I dig through cupboards I silently connect with Grandma, whose rolling pins, cutters, and tin plates help me recreate her famous pies. Like extensions of her soft hands, her tools show me what to do. Her voice is in my ear with sound advice. *Chill your dough before rolling it*, and always taste as you go.

One plum for me, one for the pie.

Pulling out the small plates and lifters, a handful of forks, and the ice cream scoop reminds me of when Mom would lay out her serving ware the night before, ensuring it was all clean and ready. Some level of formality always creeps into my entertaining, even though this gathering tonight is simple, without the pomp of a three-course meal. Just pie and ice cream. Friends and perhaps a bottle of wine. That's all. And it's plenty.

PHOTOGRAPHS BY JASON HUDSON
WORDS AND STYLING BY ASHLEY DENTON

WOOL SOCKS

I like to have presents, however small, for my guests.
Socks, particularly wool socks, are the perfect thing.

The arrival of fall (and impending winter) is always a sign that it's time to retreat—to be inside, to find comfort, to feel cozy. But it's important to me that this time also include friends, and not be a period of solitude. It's my favorite time of year to have friends over, for no other reason than to find this coziness together.

I like to have presents, however small, for my guests. Socks, particularly wool socks, are the perfect thing. I choose big chunky knits and soft cashmere wool blends in the deep earthy colors of autumn. I like to package the socks in kraft paper, tied with twine or baker's string, with the edges poking out for a bit of color. It's not a complete surprise, but it is a lovely thing to unwrap.

When my guests arrive, often with wet, cold feet or a chill in their nose, it's time for new socks and hot drinks. An old pair gets swapped out for a dry pair, and we move to the table for simple snacks like olives, pears and apples, a nice blue Morbier cheese with nutty spelt crackers, and a frittata for just a bit of saltiness. I serve hot mint tea and coffee, and sometimes even mulled cider.

We are lazy together all afternoon; it's a time for chatting, for board games, for curling up in wool blankets, and finally, for retreating to the couch. We gather with a stack of books and are absorbed by their images and words. We hold our mugs of tea, staying warm and feeling the soft wool around our toes.

PHOTOGRAPHS AND WORDS BY YOUNGNA PARK

A MOTHER'S LETTER: OUR TRADITIONS

ENTERTAINING FOR YOUNG FAMILIES

PHOTOGRAPHS AND WORDS BY EDEN LANG

Our family, our traditions – those memories will always be true.

In these cold winter mornings with the windows frosted over we seem to be in our own little world. Safe, warm, and happy. We wake, eat, brush our teeth and chase after one another. Love and life just seem to happen. Often a little stress and rush will spice things up—and then I blink—and find I'm alone with my sweet baby until we can find you two after school. What happens during those hours seems a little mysterious. I often worry about what your peers are doing and how they might be influencing you. How do we help you even more than what we have already taught you? If I could just give you a weight that might anchor you, I would. Something to remind you to always be you. Please be you. No one else. You are such amazing little people. You just need little reminders. So I try.

I try to let family traditions be an anchor in you. Because I want family to be a part of you. It is such a huge part of me. I love to wake some mornings and find ten unexpected toes snuggled in our bed. To know that every Sunday evening will bring dinner with grandparents and cousins, and to know that the chaos that comes with those evenings will be a sweet memory. I pray that every tradition, whether it involves a large family gathering or something as simple as a lazy weekend morning together, will remind you to be true to yourself. Our family, our traditions—those memories will always be true. There is a simple beauty in our family traditions. I hope they will give you strength.

Love you always, *Mom*

COLORS OF WINTER

CLOSING PHOTOGRAPH ESSAY BY ANDREA GENTL AND MARTIN HYERS

Photographers Jaquilyn and Travis Shumate

SPECIAL THANKS
Paintings Katie Stratton
Art Director at Weldon Owen Ali Zeigler
Production Director at Weldon Owen Chris Hemesath

ENTERTAINING DETAILS & COLORS OF WINTER
Photography Andrea Gentl and
Martin Hyers of Gentl and Hyers
Assist/Digi tech/Model Paola Ambrosi DeMagistris
Brooklyn, New York
Prop stylist Angharad Bailey
Brooklyn, New York
Model/Stylist Kalen Kaminski
Brooklyn, New York
Product loan Brook Farm General Store
New York, New York

ENTERTAINING DETAILS
Digi tech, Model Meredith Munn
Apron loan Libeco-Lagae
Teas Bellocq
Stash of bowls gleena ceramics
Candles Brook Farm General Store
Candlesticks Ted Muehling

COLORS OF WINTER
Frutier/Flying Fox Maggie Nescur
Charcuterie New York Farm 2 Door
New York State
Wild foods forager Evan Strusinski
Brovetto Dairy
Breuckelen Distilling Company, Inc.—Brooklyn Made
Gin
Handmade knives Cut Brooklyn
Brooklyn Butcher Blocks
Hand-dyed shibori Upstate

MEN BEHIND THE MEAL
Locations Basque Country
Boucherie Regalez-Vous
Frenchie Restaurant, *Paris*
Le Chateaubriand, *Paris*

PICNIC IN THE FOREST
Wardrobe Stylist Lauren Hartmann
Portland, Oregon

TEA FOR TWO
Antiques Bower Antiques, Quy Nguyen
Brooklyn, New York
Flowers Ariel Dearie Flowers
Brooklyn, New York

THE SEASON OF INTENTIONAL GATHERINGS
Sweater Vince
Top Miu Miu
Socks Esk Valley Knitwear
Men's Sweater Elder Statesman
Men's Shirt Levi's
Men's Jeans Levi's

WINTERS REST
Location Buchanan Log House
Nashville, TN

SUNDAY ROAST
Location The Drapers Arms
London, England

BEE HARVEST
Her apron Small Batch Production
New York
His apron Cooking Gorgeous
Cambridgeshire, England

OREGON COAST
Food Stylist Julie Pointer
Stylist Emma Robertson
Photographer Amos Lanka
Stylist Ashley Marcu
Music Andrew Stonestreet, Daniel Dixon, Catherine Feeny,
Sebastian Rogers, Michael Blake
Baking Jenny Blake
Wine Enso Winery
Portland, Oregon

WANDERERS AT THE TABLE
Location Ian Knauer farm

FORGING FAMILY
Photographer Lou Mora
Photo Assistant Justin Donias
Video Steve Pappin
Set Stylist Bash, Please
Wardrobe Stylist Gena Tuso
Wardrobe Stylist Assistant Leah Henken
Hair Anny Kim
Makeup Jennifer Fiamengo
Food Heirloom LA
Location Mcgrath Family Farm

Wardrobe
(No payments were accepted for these product placements)

Robbie:
Flannel striped shirt Steven Alan
Beanie (at dinner) Field Scout
Denim shirt Fischer
Pants Steven Alan
Shoes Clae

Steve:
Vintage military jacket available at Wasteland
Flannel shirt Penfield
Henley shirt Vince
Shoes Vans
Pants Levi's

Johnny:
Jacket Woolrich Woolen Mills
Thermal Shades of Grey
Scarf (at dinner) Vintage

Sweater Steven Alan
Shoes Vans
Jeans Levi's

Sierra:
Vintage jacket (at dinner) available at Wasteland
Button-down flannel shirt Nicholas K
Boots Vintage, stylist's own
Necklace Mineralogy
Striped tshirt Vince
Pants Vince

Stephanie:
Vintage military jacket available at Wasteland
Sweater vest (at dinner) Nicholas K
Striped shirt Steven Alan
Boots Love Label
Poncho Levi's
Jeans Levi's

Alexa:
Utility poncho (at dinner) Steven Alan
Scarf (at dinner) Symmetry Goods
Collared shirt BB Dakota
Burgundy sweater Vince
Socks American Apparel
Boots The Generic Man
Trousers Steven Alan

Makeup Mac Cosmetics & Dermalogica Skincare
Los Angeles, California

WARMTH OF THE INVERTED YEAR
Stylist Adelaide Brown
Greensboro, North Carolina

BEFORE COMPANY
Props Rustica Tabletop
Toronto, Canada

WOOL SOCKS
Wool products ESK Valley Knitwear
Annan, Scotland

CLOSING PHOTO
Photographer Jaquilyn and Travis Shumate
Tacoma, Washington

COVER PHOTO
Photographer Jessica Peterson
Salt Lake City, Utah

SOURCES
1. Robinson, Marilynne. *Housekeeping* (Toronto, Canada: Harper Perennial, 1980), 62.

2. Bradbury, Ray. *Dandelion Wine* (Bantam Books, 1976).

3. Robbins, John. *May All Be Fed* (Avon, 1993).

4. Cowper, William. "The Winter Evening," *The Task*.

KEEP IN TOUCH